Just Spelling

Louis Fidge

Approach to spelling

This series is based on the statutory curriculum requirements and objectives. It encourages pupils to use a variety of approaches including:

- *auditory*: using the phonological system of our language to analyse and build up words; using analogy to generalise what they have learnt to other words with similar sound patterns; using rhyming and syllabification

- *visual*: developing the habit of looking carefully at, and analysing the structure of, words; looking for common letter patterns; looking for smaller words within longer words

- *tactile*: meaningful writing activities to help children get 'the feel' of words and letter patterns

- *meaning*: understanding word meanings, roots and etymology; setting words in appropriate sentences; understanding the grammatical structure of words by breaking them down into morphemes where appropriate (prefixes, suffixes etc.)

Key features

Unit number and title

Key to spelling
Introduction and explanation of key spelling point with clear example and supporting illustration. It is suggested that this section is discussed fully with the class as a whole, to ensure the key spelling point is understood.

Practice
This section involves a variety of activities encouraging children to make and use words exemplifying the key spelling point of the unit. This section may be tackled by the class as a whole, by groups or by children working independently. It is important that children are encouraged to discuss words introduced and to use them in context to ensure their meaning is understood.

Extension
This offers activities of a more challenging nature, which extend and consolidate the concepts and spelling patterns being taught. This section may be tackled by the class as a whole, by groups or by children working independently.

Scope and sequence
Page 64 shows the scope and sequence, objectives and strategies used in each unit.

Fold-over flap
The unique fold-over flap at the back of the book allows the test words to be covered up for testing purposes. Children are encouraged to use the Look-Say-Cover-Write-Check method for learning the test words.

Assessment
Each unit contains a number of test words to assess children's success in understanding the key spelling point. These always appear on the right hand side of each double page spread. The test may be carried out by the teacher with the whole class or group, or by pairs of children testing each other. Children may also assess themselves individually if preferred.

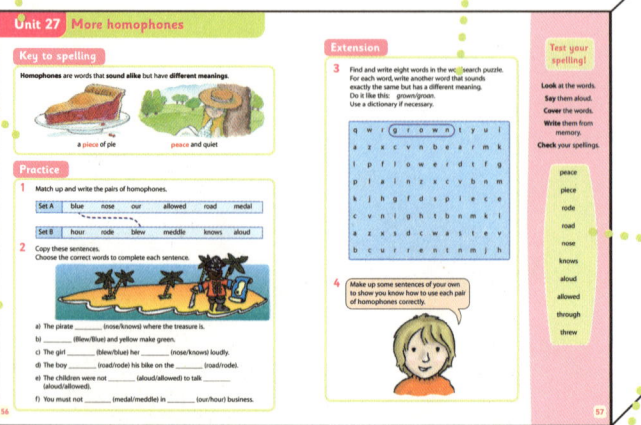

Contents

Unit	Title	Page
1	Word building (single-letter phonemes)	4
2	Word building (multiple-letter phonemes)	6
3	Same sound/different phoneme	8
4	Proofreading for mistakes	10
5	Same phoneme/different sound	12
6	Check the vowel sounds	14
7	Working out the syllables	16
8	Two-syllable words (containing a long vowel)	18
9	Regular verb endings (1)	20
10	Regular verb endings (2)	22
11	The past tense of irregular verbs	24
12	Common word endings	26
13	Spelling investigation (letter **k**)	28
14	Spelling investigation (**wa** and **wo**)	30
15	Spelling investigation (**gu**)	32
16	Spelling investigation (**se**)	34
17	Suffix -**ment**	36
18	Suffixes -**tion** and -**sion**	38
19	Suffixes -**able** and -**ible**	40
20	Suffixes -**ship**, -**hood** and -**ness**	42
21	Suffixes -**ic** and -**ive**	44
22	Suffix -**ous**	46
23	Prefixes **fore**- and **over**-	48
24	Extending words	50
25	Words with common roots	52
26	Confusing homophones	54
27	More homophones	56
28	Compound words	58
29	Tricky words!	60
30	High frequency words	62
	Scope and sequence	64

Unit 1 Word building (single-letter phonemes)

Key to spelling

Words are made up of sounds called **phonemes**.
Some phonemes are **single letters**.

van

v → a → n

belt

b → e → l → t

Practice

1 Make some words.

a) c → a → p   b) l → e → g   c) b → i → n

d) m → a → s → k   e) h → a → n → d   f) c → l → a → p

g) p → r → a → m   h) t → w → i → g

2 Write the word that goes with each picture.

a)    b)    c)    d)

e)    f)    g)    h)

Extension

3 Make each word.
Then write the word the other way round.
The first one has been done for you.

a) t → o → p

   top   pot

b) b → a → t → s

c) g → o → l → f

d) m → u → g

e) p → a → n

f) b → u → t

g) g → a → s

h) s → p → o → t

i) g → u → l → p

j) p → i → n → s

k) p → e → t → s

l) p → i → t

m) d → o → g

4  Can you think of any words that are spelt the same forwards and backwards, e.g. *pip*?

Test your spelling!

Look at the words.
Say them aloud.
Cover the words.
Write them from memory.
Check your spellings.

bag

pet

hum

gift

golf

rent

skip

slot

drag

blend

Unit 2 Word building (multiple-letter phonemes)

Key to spelling

A phoneme may be made of **one or more letters**.
To **spell** simple words you need to work out what **phonemes** they contain.

boat

b → oa → t

chair

ch → air

Practice

1 Make some words.

a) f → l → y

b) p → ai → n → t

c) b → u → ll

d) l → igh → t

e) m → ou → se

f) s → oa → p

g) b → r → ea → d

h) c → l → aw

i) m → oo → n

2 Write the word that goes with each picture.

a)

b)

c)

d)

e)

f)

g)

h)

i)

Extension

3 Choose the correct phoneme to complete each word. Use a dictionary if necessary.

a) g____t (oa/ow)

b) p____d (ay/ai)

c) ____ief (wh/th)

d) gl____ (ew/ue)

e) tr____ (igh/y)

f) sh____p (ee/ea)

g) f____d (ew/oo)

h) h____t (er/ur)

i) b____l (oi/oy)

j) y____d (ar/or)

k) f____ll (u/oo)

l) m____ (au/ore)

m) r____nd (ow/ou)

n) k____b (er/ir)

o) h____ (ear/eer)

Test your spelling!

Look at the words.
Say them aloud.
Cover the words.
Write them from memory.
Check your spellings.

beat

crew

toy

crown

road

drain

sport

sauce

bright

stood

Unit 3 Same sound/different phoneme

Key to spelling

Take care! The **phonemes** in some words **sound similar** but have **different spelling patterns**.

a n**ur**se in a sk**ir**t with a lant**er**n

Practice

1

Copy the words. Underline the **er**, **ir** or **ur** in each.

stir	term	fur	third	nerve
nurse	perch	curl	burst	girl
church	person	first	perhaps	birth
jerk	turtle	squirt	servant	curve

2 Draw a chart like this and write the words in the correct columns.

er words	**ir** words	**ur** words

8

Extension

3 Write the **er** word that means:

a) to tug

b) maybe

c) someone who serves

d) a length of time

4 Write the **ir** word that means:

a) to spray with water

b) the position before second

c) the position after second

d) being born

5 Write the **ur** word that means:

a) to break or pop

b) an animal with a shell

c) a place of worship

d) someone who cares for the sick

Test your spelling!

Look at the words.
Say them aloud.
Cover the words.
Write them from memory.
Check your spellings.

herb

verse

perfect

firm

thirty

whirl

birth

turf

purse

urchin

Unit 4 Proofreading for mistakes

Key to spelling

It is important that you **check your spellings** for silly **mistakes**.

au   or   aw
P~~aw~~l had a sh~~au~~t str~~or~~.

P**au**l had a sh**or**t str**aw**.

*Use a **dictionary** if you are not sure!*

Practice

1 Do these phoneme sums.

a) s + aw

b) h + aw + k

c) s + au + c + er

d) l + au + n + ch

e) t + or + ch

f) h + or + n

2 Choose the correct word for each picture.

a) tauch / torch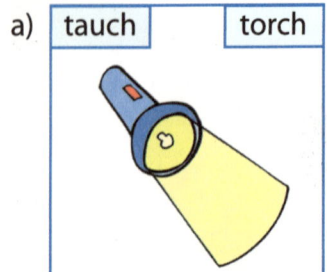

b) saucer / sawcer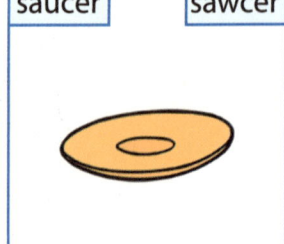

c) sor / saw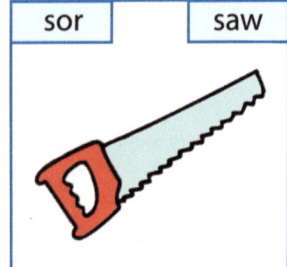

d) lawnch / launch

e) horn / haun

f) hauk / hawk

Extension

3 Write each word correctly.
Use a dictionary if necessary.

a) stawk

b) porse

c) craul

d) sorce

e) tawn

f) stawy

g) tornt

h) daun

i) nawth

j) thor

k) lawndry

l) jor

m) awthor

n) cawner

o) orful

Test your spelling!

Look at the words.
Say them aloud.
Cover the words.
Write them from memory.
Check your spellings.

ca**u**se

autumn

exh**au**sted

r**aw**

scr**aw**l

l**aw**n

c**or**d

sp**or**t

st**or**m

m**or**ning

4 Write the words you made above in sets.

au words	**aw** words	**or** words

Unit 5 Same phoneme/different sound

Key to spelling

The **phonemes** in some words **are spelt the same** but have **different sounds**.

He is r**ea**ding a book.

This **ea** has a **long** vowel sound.

She bumped her h**ea**d.

This **ea** has a **short** vowel sound.

Practice

1 Make some **ea** words with a **long** vowel sound.

n**ea**t   h___p   sp___k   t___m   b___ch

2 Write some **ea** words with a **short** vowel sound.

br**ea**d   d___f   sw___t   w___ther   m___dow

3 Make some **oo** words with a **long** vowel sound.

f**oo**d   st___l   h___p   pr___f   br___m

4 Write some **oo** words with a **short** vowel sound.

g**oo**d   b___k   f___t   st___d   sh___k

12

Extension

5 Divide these words into two sets according to the sound the **y** phoneme makes.

baby　　cry

why　　lady

reply　　copy

lorry　　supply

tiny　　multiply

shy　　sunny

6 Copy these **ow** words. Add some more of your own. Divide them into two sets according to the sound the **ow** phoneme makes.

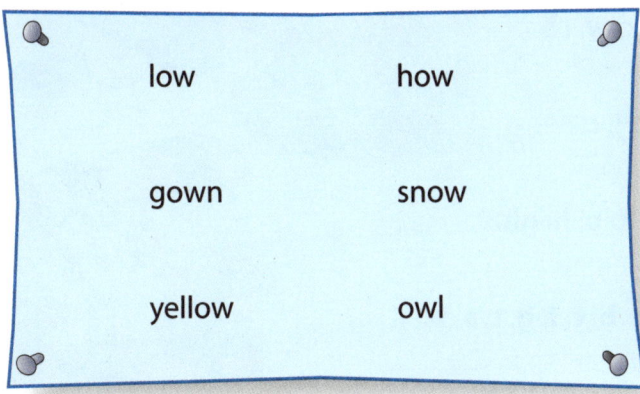

low　　how

gown　　snow

yellow　　owl

Test your spelling!

Look at the words.
Say them aloud.
Cover the words.
Write them from memory.
Check your spellings.

Which of these words contain long vowel phonemes? Which contain short vowel phonemes?

f**ea**st

tr**ea**d

sw**oo**p

cr**oo**k

dr**y**

bab**y**

thr**ow**

h**ow**l

w**ear**

cl**ear**

13

Unit 6 Check the vowel sounds

Key to spelling

Sometimes the vowels **i** and **o** make a **long vowel sound** and **say their names** when they come **before nd**, **ld**, **lt** or **st** in words.

a k**i**nd ch**i**ld

an **o**ld gh**o**st

Practice

1 Make some new words.

a) Change the **m** in **m**ind to **k, b, f, w**.

b) Change the **bl** in **bl**ind to **gr, beh, rem**.

c) Change the **m** in **m**ild to **w, ch**.

d) Change the **b** in **b**olt to **j, c**.

e) Change the **m** in **m**ost to **p, h, gh**.

f) Change the **h** in **h**old to **b, c, f, g, t, s, sc**.

a b**o**ld pirate burying some g**o**ld

14

Extension

2 Use the words you made in question 1.
Write the word that means the opposite of:

a) untie

b) being able to see

c) lose

d) unkind

e) in front of

f) adult

g) tame

h) hot

i) bought

j) unfold

k) let go of

l) least

3 Copy these words. Underline the odd word out.

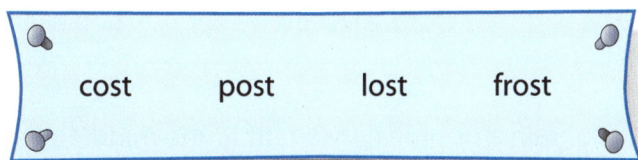

cost   post   lost   frost

4 We can pronounce 'wind' in two different ways. Make up two sentences of your own. Use the word in both ways.

Test your spelling!

Look at the words.
Say them aloud.
Cover the words.
Write them from memory.
Check your spellings.

blind

behind

remind

child

wild

bold

scold

bolt

most

ghost

Unit 7 — Working out the syllables

Key to spelling

When we say a word **slowly** we can hear how many **beats** or **syllables** it has. You can **tap out** the syllables of a word as you say it to help you.

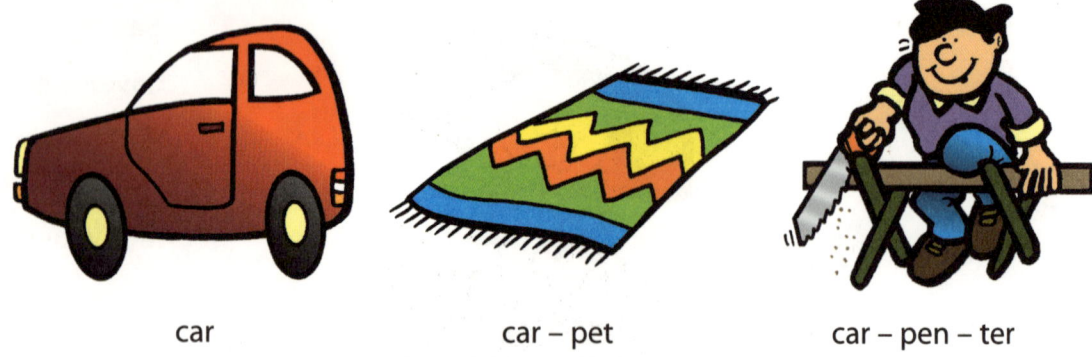

car

car – pet

car – pen – ter

This has **1** syllable.

This has **2** syllables.

This has **3** syllables.

Practice

1 Say each word slowly.
Write and say if it contains **1**, **2** or **3** syllables.

a) modern 2	f) sport	k) expensive	p) direct
b) invade	g) farm	l) September	q) together
c) cabin	h) bird	m) travel	r) introduce
d) king	i) industry	n) habit	s) damage
e) determine	j) seat	o) method	t) perfectly

2 These two-syllable words all contain a double consonant in the middle. Break them down into syllables. Do it like this: *rubble = rub – ble*

a) hobby   d) raffle   g) giggle

b) follow   e) apple   h) hurry

c) assist   f) bottle   i) dazzle

Extension

3 Write the days of the week that contain:

　　a) two syllables　　　　b) three syllables

4 Write the name of each day and break it into syllables.

　Do it like this: *Sun – day*

5 Write the months of the year that contain:

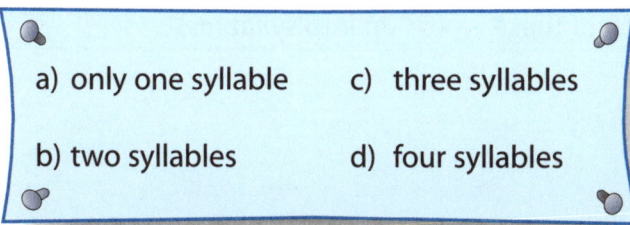

　　a) only one syllable　　c) three syllables

　　b) two syllables　　　　d) four syllables

6 Write the months of the year that have more than one syllable.
Break each name down into syllables.

　Do it like this: *A – pril*

7 Write the names of ten children in your class. Break their names down into syllables.

Test your spelling!

Look at the words.

Say them aloud.

Cover the words.

Write them from memory.

Check your spellings.

How many syllables does each of these words contain?

ro – bot

rab – bit

be – gin

nim – ble

sud – den – ly

bi – cy – cle

im – por – tant

dif – fer – ent – ly

cat – er – pil – lar

in – tro – duc – tion

17

Unit 8 Two-syllable words (containing a long vowel)

Key to spelling

lady
la – dy

tiger
ti – ger

robot
ro – bot

> When we say a word we usually **stress** one syllable more than another. In the words above we stress the **first** syllable.
> The **vowel** in the first syllable of each of these words has a **long** sound.
> Notice how we split each of these words up into syllables.

Practice

1 Do these syllable sums.

a) gra + vy
b) e + vil
c) i + rate
d) stu + pid
e) se + cret
f) pi + lot
g) po + em
h) hu + man
i) a + corn
j) spi + der
k) o + pen
l) u + nit

2 Write the word above that means:

a) something you do not tell anyone

b) an animal that spins a web

c) someone who flies planes

d) something from which oak trees grow

e) very bad

f) a sauce you pour on your dinner

g) not shut

h) not clever

Extension

3 Divide these words into syllables.
Do it like this: *basin = ba – sin*

a) holy

b) crocus

c) pupil

d) even

e) humid

f) diet

g) duty

h) rival

i) private

j) later

4 Match up the first and second syllables to make some words. Write the words you make.

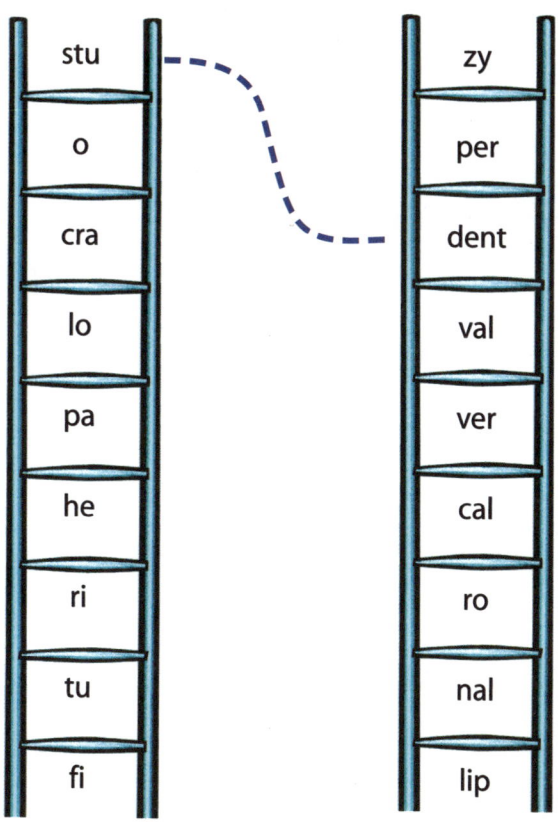

Test your spelling!

Look at the words.

Say them aloud.

Cover the words.

Write them from memory.

Check your spellings.

ba – sin

pu – pil

si – lent

cra – zy

vi – tal

po – ny

spi – der

ti – ger

la – dy

va – cant

Unit 9 — Regular verb endings (1)

Key to spelling

The spelling of **regular verbs** follows a **clear pattern**.

act – acting – acted   bake – baking – baked   hop – hopping – hopped

Rule 1
With many verbs we can just add an ending **without changing** the **root verb**.

Rule 2
If the verb **ends** with a **consonant + e** we **drop the e** before we add the ending.

Rule 3
If the verb has **one syllable** and **ends** with a **short vowel** sound followed by a **consonant** we **double** the final **consonant**.

Practice

1 Use **Rule 1** to help you spell some regular verbs. Copy and fill in this chart.

Root verb	+ ending **ing**	+ ending **ed**
brush		
climb		
dress		

2 Now copy and fill in this chart. Use **Rule 2** to help.

Root verb	+ ending **ing**	+ ending **ed**
skate		
dine		
joke		

Extension

3 The verb in each sentence is incorrect.
Rewrite each sentence correctly.
Use **Rule 3** to help you.

a) We claped loudly at the end of the show.

b) I was huming a tune.

c) I am stoping in tonight.

d) The trainers fited me very well.

e) I huged my mum tightly.

f) The old man ploded along slowly.

g) The hare was runing very fast.

h) My dog waged its tail happily.

i) It was geting very dark.

j) I ziped up my jacket.

4 Take off the ending of each verb.
Write the root verb you are left with.
Do it like this: *popped – pop*

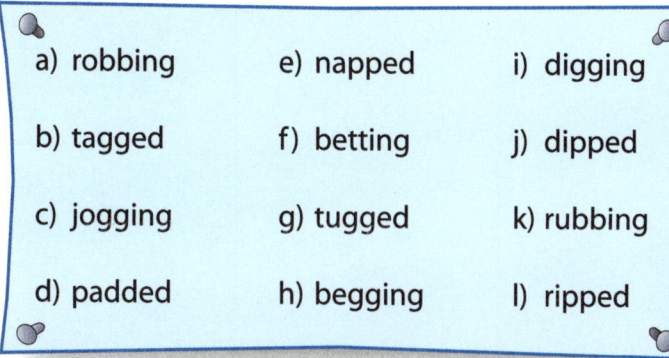

a) robbing
b) tagged
c) jogging
d) padded
e) napped
f) betting
g) tugged
h) begging
i) digging
j) dipped
k) rubbing
l) ripped

Test your spelling!

Look at the words.
Say them aloud.
Cover the words.
Write them from memory.
Check your spellings.

Which rule does each of these verbs follow?

walking

smiling

closing

napping

bobbing

talked

wiped

amused

pinned

hummed

21

Unit 10 Regular verb endings (2)

Key to spelling

The spelling of **regular verbs** follows a **clear pattern**. Many verbs end with a **consonant + y**.

hurry – hurries   hurry – hurrying   hurry – hurried

Rule 1
When we add **s** we change the **y** to **i** and add **es**.

Rule 2
We can add **ing** without changing the spelling of the root verb.

Rule 3
When we add **ed** we change the **y** to **i** and add **ed**.

Practice

1 Copy and complete this chart.

Root verb	+ ending s	+ ending ing	+ ending ed
carry			
marry			
try			
copy			
worry			
empty			
cry			
apply			

Extension

2 The verb in each sentence is incorrect.
Rewrite each sentence correctly.

a) The prince marryed the princess.

b) Anna always trys hard.

c) A plane flys high in the sky.

d) I replyed to the invitation.

e) A towel drys you.

f) 2 multiplyed by 4 is 8.

g) A baby often crys.

h) I emptyed the glass in one gulp.

i) Tom relys on Anna a lot.

3 Take off the ending of each verb.
Write the root verb you are left with.
Do it like this: *cried – cry*

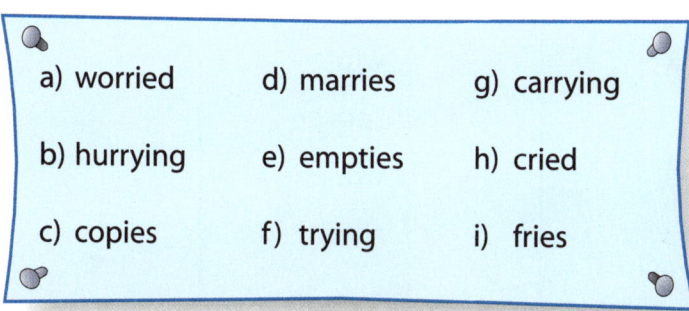

a) worried   d) marries   g) carrying

b) hurrying e) empties   h) cried

c) copies   f) trying   i) fries

Test your spelling!

Look at the words.
Say them aloud.
Cover the words.
Write them from memory.
Check your spellings.

crying

flying

trying

copies

empties

relies

applied

carried

hurried

multiplied

Unit 11 The past tense of irregular verbs

Key to spelling

The spelling of the **past tense** of **irregular verbs** is sometimes surprising and does **not** follow a **clear pattern**.

caught
The girl ~~catched~~ a cold.

catch ⟶ caught
(verb)   (past tense)

wore
The boy ~~weared~~ his new trainers.

wear ⟶ wore
(verb)   (past tense)

Practice

1 Match up the present tense of each verb with its past tense.
Do it like this: *take – took*

present tense	past tense
drive	sang
go	knew
sing	drove
wind	hurt
write	went
know	wrote
hurt	spoke
see	wound
speak	stole
steal	saw

Extension

2 Change the underlined irregular verb into the past tense. The first one has been done for you.

a) I <u>teach</u> my dog some tricks.

I taught my dog some tricks.

b) My parents <u>give</u> me some pocket money.

c) They <u>leave</u> at seven o'clock.

d) We <u>swim</u> in the sea.

e) Ben <u>hides</u> from Amy.

f) I <u>grow</u> vegetables in my garden.

g) Sam <u>is</u> often late.

h) Mrs Jones <u>feels</u> ill.

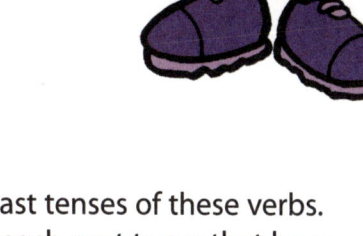

3 Copy the present and past tenses of these verbs. Underline the letters in each past tense that have changed.
The first one has been done for you.

a) come – c<u>a</u>me

b) kneel – knelt

c) grow – grew

d) fly – flew

e) sing – sang

f) seek – sought

g) break – broke

h) deal – dealt

Test your spelling!

Look at the words.
Say them aloud.
Cover the words.
Write them from memory.
Check your spellings.

taught

knew

gave

chose

bought

rode

left

forgot

ate

began

Unit 12 Common word endings

Key to spelling

Look for **common letter strings** at the **end** of words.
Use them to help you spell other words.

a br**ight** l**ight** at n**ight**

Practice

1 Make some words with common endings. Write the words in your book.

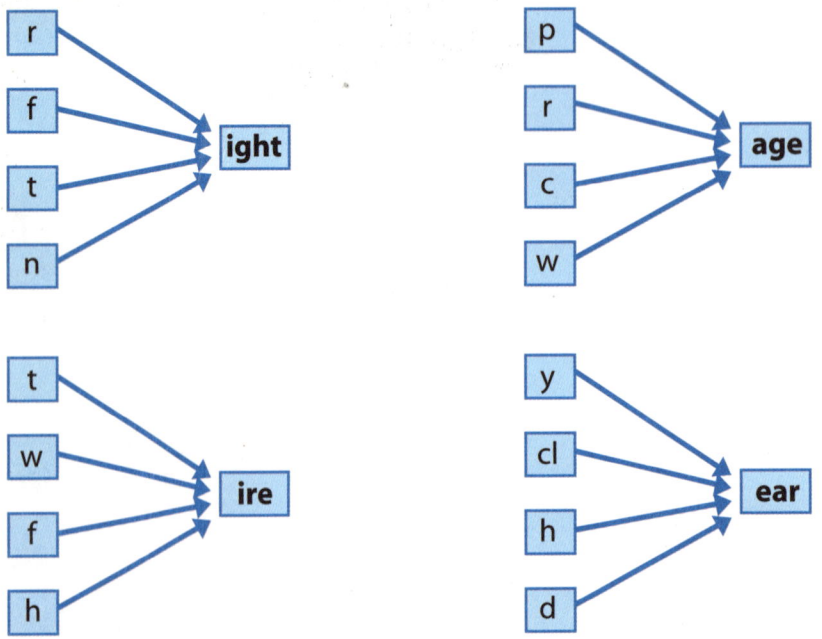

2 Now write each set of words you made again, in alphabetical order.

Extension

3 Make some new words, with the same ending.

a) Change the **l** in **l**edge to **w**, **h**, **sl**.

b) Change the **d** in **d**itch to **h**, **p**, **w**, **st**.

c) Change the **c** in **c**are to **d**, **r**, **sh**, **bew**.

d) Change the **m** in **m**ore to **c**, **b**, **t**, **sc**.

e) Change the **d** in **d**ue to **bl**, **gl**, **cl**, **tr**.

f) Change the **l** in **l**ie to **p**, **d**, **t**.

g) Change the **t** in **t**oe to **f**, **d**, **r**, **w**.

h) Change the **c** in **c**ure to **s**, **l**, **p**, **inj**.

i) Change the **p** in **p**ace to **f**, **r**, **gr**, **sp**.

j) Change the **s** in **s**our to **h**, **fl**, **sc**.

4 Now write each set of words you made in question 3 again, in alphabetical order.

Test your spelling!

Look at the words.
Say them aloud.
Cover the words.
Write them from memory.
Check your spellings.

mi**ght**

fri**ght**

p**age**

enr**age**

d**ear**

app**ear**

f**etch**

sk**etch**

br**idge**

fr**idge**

Unit 13 Spelling investigation (letter k)

Key to spelling

The letters **c** and **k** often make the **same sound** in words. The letter **c** is the most **common** but sometimes we **need** to use the letter **k**.

chick

a **k**ettle in a **k**itchen

a shar**k** in a tan**k**

| We cannot end short one-syllable words with **c**, so we use **ck**. | We need **k** before the vowels **e** and **i**. | We use **k** after another consonant if it comes at the **end** of a word. |

Practice

1 Make some words.

```
         ck
ba_ck_    pa____    sa____    de____    pe____

         ck
si____    ki____    lo____    ro____    lu____
```

2 Copy this chart. Fill it in with the words you made in question 1.

ack words	**eck** words	**ick** words	**ock** words	**uck** words

Extension

3 Match each word in the box to its meaning. Use a dictionary if necessary.

kennel	kerb	kernel
kestrel	ketchup	keg
kipper	kidnap	kilt
kindle	kiln	kiwi

a) a smoked herring

b) a tartan skirt

c) a shelter for a dog

d) a large oven or furnace

e) the inner part of a nut

f) a New Zealand bird that cannot fly

g) to set fire to

h) the edge of the pavement

i) a sauce made from tomatoes

j) to take a person by force

k) a small cask

l) a bird of prey

4 Think of two words that end with each of the following pairs of letters:

a) **sk**   b) **lk**   c) **nk**   d) **rk**

Test your spelling!

Look at the words.
Say them aloud.
Cover the words.
Write them from memory.
Check your spellings.

stick

check

kettle

key

kink

task

mask

talk

think

park

Unit 14 Spelling investigation (wa and wo)

Key to spelling

The vowels **a** and **o** do not behave as expected after the letter **w**.

a sw**a**n in a sw**a**mp

The letter **a** is often pronounced like **o** when it comes after **w**.

a w**o**nderful w**o**lf

The letter **o** may be pronounced in several different ways after **w**.

Practice

1 Make some words.

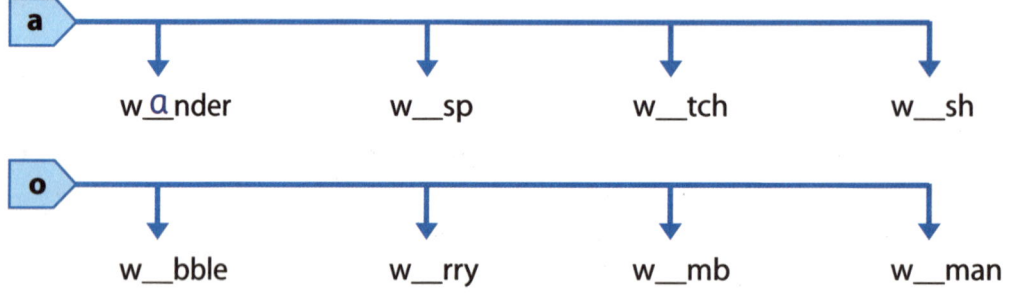

w_a_nder   w__sp   w__tch   w__sh

w__bble   w__rry   w__mb   w__man

2 Write each set of words you made in alphabetical order.

3 Which word means:

a) the opposite of man

b) to rock unsteadily

c) the place where a baby grows

d) a flying insect that stings

e) like a small clock

f) to walk about in a slow manner

g) to make something clean with water

h) to be afraid something will go wrong

Extension

> When **ar** comes after **w** it sounds like **or**.
> When **or** comes after **w** it sounds like **er**!

4 Choose **ar** or **or** to complete each word. Use a dictionary if necessary.

a) w___m   quite hot

b) sw___m   a large number of insects

c) w___ld   the earth

d) w___se   less good

e) w___n   to tell someone of danger

f) w___k   a job

g) w___th   to have a certain value

h) w___d   a group of letters

i) w___m   lives in the soil

Test your spelling!

Look at the words.
Say them aloud.
Cover the words.
Write them from memory.
Check your spellings.

w**a**sp

w**a**tch

w**o**man

w**o**mbat

w**o**nder

w**or**m

w**or**k

w**or**d

w**ar**m

rew**ar**d

31

Unit 15 Spelling investigation (gu)

Key to spelling

The letter **g** usually makes a **hard** sound in words (as in **g**ate and **g**o).
To keep its hard sound we often put **u** after **g** when it comes before **e** or **i**.

guess

guitar

Practice

1 Make some words. Write them in your book.

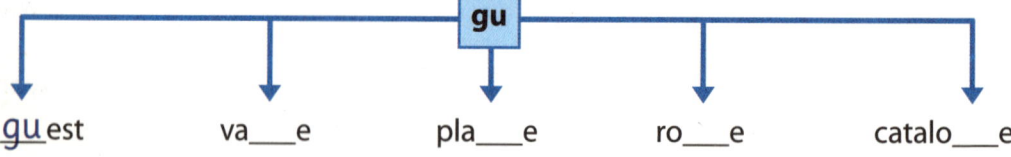

<u>gu</u>est   va___e   pla___e   ro___e   catalo___e

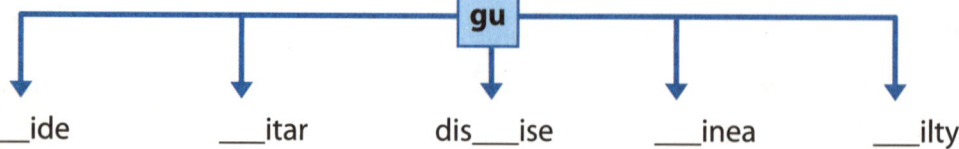

___ide   ___itar   dis___ise   ___inea   ___ilty

2 Write the **gu** words with:

a) five letters   b) six letters   c) more than six letters

3 Write the meaning of the words in the wall below.

Use a dictionary if necessary.

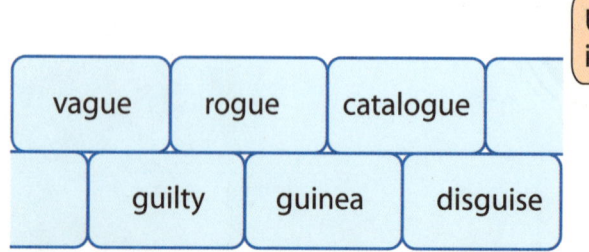

| vague | rogue | catalogue |
| guilty | guinea | disguise |

Extension

4 Use the following words correctly in sentences of your own:

> league   tongue
>
> intrigue   dialogue

5 Here are some words that do not follow the **gu** rule. Write them in alphabetical order.

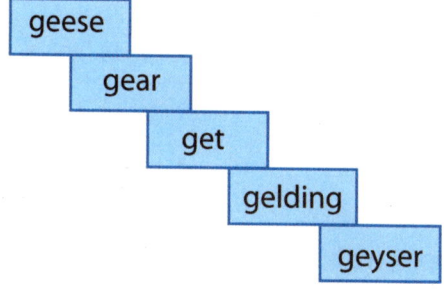

geese
gear
get
gelding
geyser

6 Here are some more words that do not follow the **gu** rule. Write them in alphabetical order.

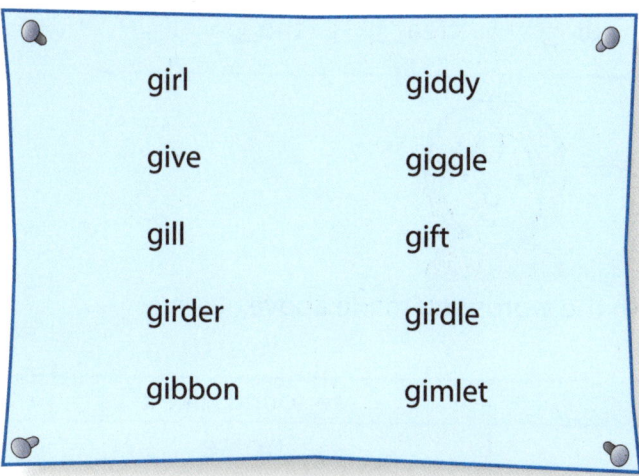

girl   giddy

give   giggle

gill   gift

girder   girdle

gibbon   gimlet

Test your spelling!

Look at the words.
Say them aloud.
Cover the words.
Write them from memory.
Check your spellings.

guess

guest

guilty

guide

guitar

guillotine

ro**gu**e

va**gu**e

lea**gu**e

dis**gu**ise

33

Unit 16 Spelling investigation (se)

Key to spelling

The letters **se** at the end of single-syllable words can be pronounced in **two** different ways.

mou**se**

Here the **se** sounds like **s**.

chee**se**

Here the **se** sounds like **z**.

Practice

1. Copy the words and complete each word with **se**.

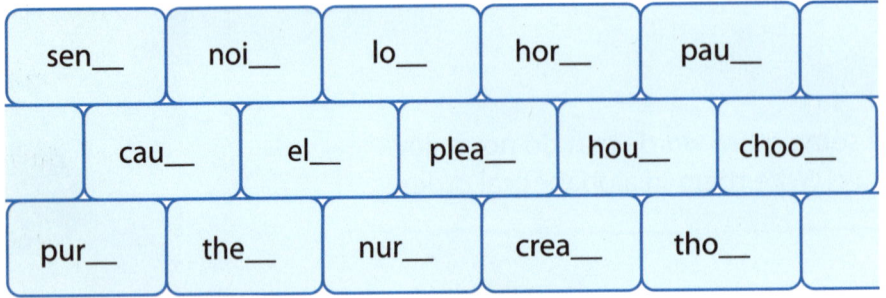

sen__   noi__   lo__   hor__   pau__

cau__   el__   plea__   hou__   choo__

pur__   the__   nur__   crea__   tho__

2.  Say each word and listen carefully to the **se** sound.

Copy this chart. Fill it in with the words you made above.

se sounds like s	se sounds like z
sense	noise

Extension

3 Copy each sentence.
Fill in each gap with a word ending in **se**.

a) You keep money in a _____.

b) A hubbub is a lot of _____.

c) A _____ has four hoofs.

d) A _____ squeaks.

e) _____ is made from milk.

f) A _____ looks after sick people.

g) I like to _____ new clothes for myself.

h) I folded the paper to make a _____ in it.

i) To _____ is to make something happen.

j) It is polite to say _____ when you ask for something.

k) The bright child had a lot of good _____.

4 Copy this silly sentence. Underline the four words in it that end in **ze** and break the **se** rule.

> The cold breeze makes me freeze and sneeze and wheeze.

Test your spelling!

Look at the words.
Say them aloud.
Cover the words.
Write them from memory.
Check your spellings.

sen**se**

hor**se**

mou**se**

pur**se**

crea**se**

poi**se**

plea**se**

lo**se**

tho**se**

chee**se**

Unit 17 Suffix -ment

Key to spelling

A **suffix** is a **group of letters** that may be added to the **end** of a word. When you add a suffix it **changes** the **meaning** or **job** of the **root** word.

When you **agree** about something you come to an **agreement**.

agree (verb) + ment (suffix) = agree**ment** (noun)

Practice

1 Copy and complete this chart. Change the verbs to nouns by adding the suffix **ment**.

verbs	nouns
entertain	entertainment
amuse	
improve	
employ	
astonish	

2 Copy and complete this chart. Take the suffix off each noun and write the verb from which the noun comes.

verbs	nouns
	enjoyment
	arrangement
	management
	commencement
	encouragement
	movement

36

Extension

3 Write the **ment** words from questions 1 and 2 that have:

a) 2 syllables

b) 3 syllables

c) 4 syllables

4 Here are some tricky **ment** words. Copy each word. Write and say what you think is tricky about its spelling.

government	parliament
environment	judgment
argument	advertisement

5 Make up some sentences of your own. Use the **ment** words in question 4 in them.

Test your spelling!

Look at the words.
Say them aloud.
Cover the words.
Write them from memory.
Check your spellings.

move**ment**

enjoy**ment**

entertain**ment**

agree**ment**

amuse**ment**

astonish**ment**

encourage**ment**

argu**ment**

advertise**ment**

govern**ment**

Unit 18 Suffixes -tion and -sion

Key to spelling

When you add a suffix it sometimes **changes** the **spelling** of the **root word** slightly.

educate (verb) + tion (suffix)

= educa**tion** (noun)

explode (verb) + sion (suffix)

= explo**sion** (noun)

The suffix **tion** at the end of a word sounds like **shun**.

The suffix **sion** at the end of a word sounds like **zhun**.

Practice

1 Join up each **tion** noun to the verb from which it comes. Write the pairs of words in your book.

verbs	nouns
create	decoration
examine	action
decorate	creation
inform	inspection
act	preparation
inspect	examination
protect	information
prepare	competition
compete	protection

2 Join up each **sion** noun to the verb from which it comes. Write the pairs of words in your book.

verbs	nouns
include	confusion
invade	decision
confuse	division
divide	inclusion
conclude	television
decide	invasion
televise	erosion
revise	conclusion
erode	revision

Extension

3 Write the **tion** word from question 1 that means:

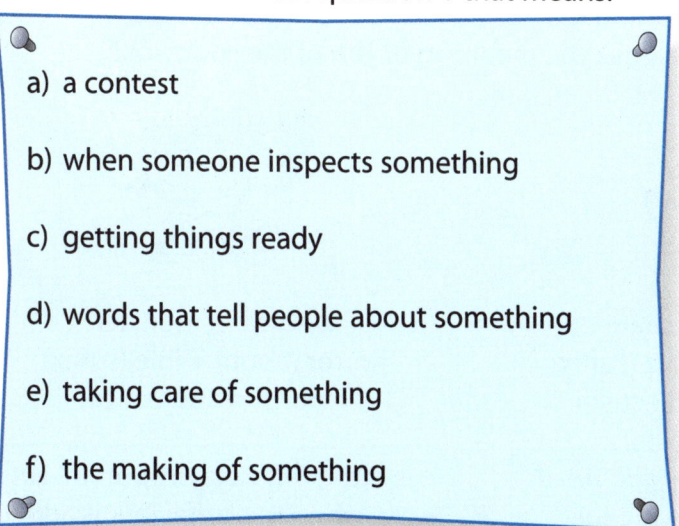

a) a contest

b) when someone inspects something

c) getting things ready

d) words that tell people about something

e) taking care of something

f) the making of something

4 Write the **sion** word from question 2 that means:

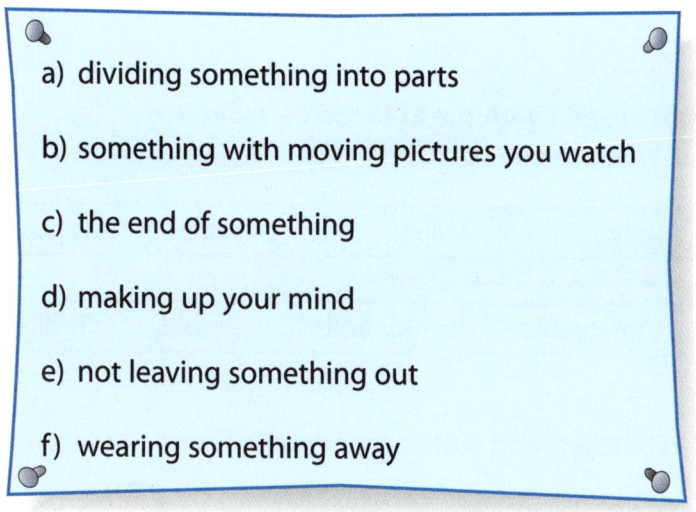

a) dividing something into parts

b) something with moving pictures you watch

c) the end of something

d) making up your mind

e) not leaving something out

f) wearing something away

5 Copy these words carefully.
Write a sentence to say what you notice about them.

admission	permission
expression	discussion
possession	profession

Test your spelling!

Look at the words.
Say them aloud.
Cover the words.
Write them from memory.
Check your spellings.

collec**tion**

direc**tion**

forma**tion**

opera**tion**

exhibi**tion**

televi**sion**

deci**sion**

inva**sion**

explo**sion**

divi**sion**

Unit 19 Suffixes -able and -ible

Key to spelling

A **suffix** is a **group of letters** that may be added to the **end** of a word. When you add a suffix it **changes** the **meaning** or **job** of the **root** word.

a comfort**able** chair
comfort (noun) + able (suffix)
= comfort**able** (adjective)

a horr**ible** monster
horror (noun) + ible (suffix)
= horr**ible** (adjective)

It is **easy** to spot the **root word** when the suffix **able** is added.

It is often **difficult** to spot the **root word** when the suffix **ible** is added.

Practice

1 Match up the root words in Set A with the **able** words in Set B from which they come. Write the pairs of words in your book.

Set A	fashion	rely	value	credit	notice

Set B	valuable	noticeable	fashionable	reliable	creditable

2 Add **able** to the word in brackets and write each sentence correctly.

a) The scientist made a (remark) discovery.

b) I felt (miser) when I was ill.

c) The girl wore (suit) trainers for running.

d) The toy was a (reason) price.

e) Anna is a (depend) girl.

40

Extension

3 Choose **able** or **ible** to complete each word. Use a dictionary if necessary.

a) valu_____

b) poss_____

c) obtain_____

d) reli_____

e) vis_____

f) respons_____

g) manage_____

h) flex_____

i) terr_____

j) consider_____

k) incred_____

l) horr_____

m) sens_____

n) remark_____

o) punish_____

p) revers_____

Test your spelling!

Look at the words.
Say them aloud.
Cover the words.
Write them from memory.
Check your spellings.

comfort**able**

reason**able**

suit**able**

reli**able**

valu**able**

horr**ible**

terr**ible**

invis**ible**

flex**ible**

sens**ible**

41

Unit 20: Suffixes -ship, -hood and -ness

Key to spelling

A **suffix** is a **group of letters** that may be added to the **end** of a word. When you add a suffix it **changes** the **meaning** or **job** of the **root** word.

The man was very **ill**.
His **illness** was very serious.

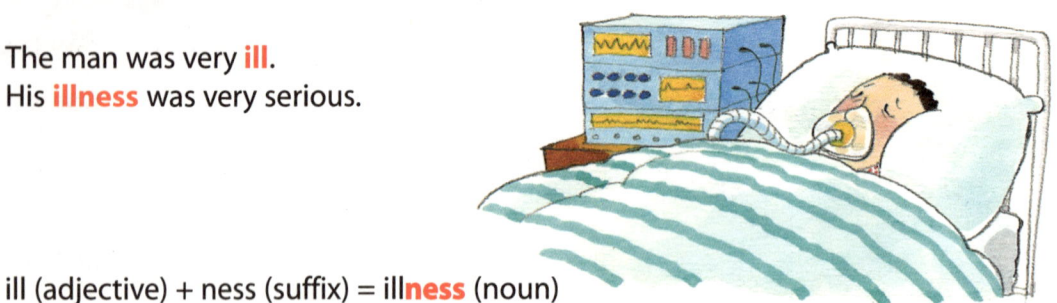

ill (adjective) + ness (suffix) = ill**ness** (noun)

Practice

1 Make some words by adding suffixes.

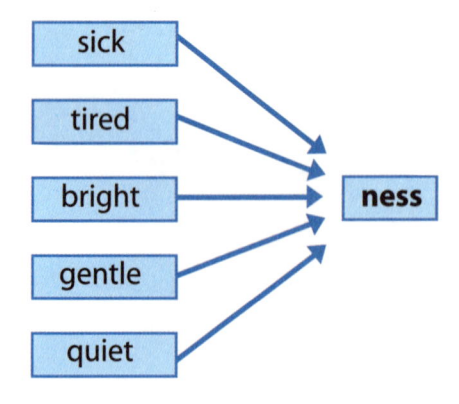

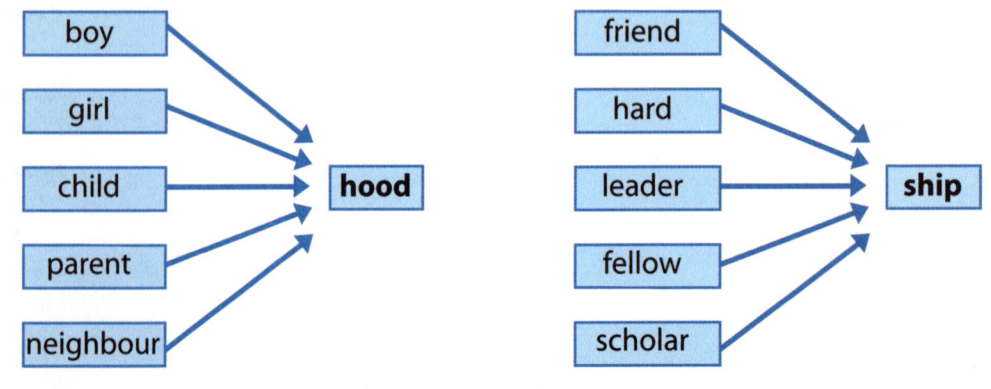

- sick
- tired
- bright → **ness**
- gentle
- quiet

- boy
- girl
- child → **hood**
- parent
- neighbour

- friend
- hard
- leader → **ship**
- fellow
- scholar

2 Now write each set of words you made in alphabetical order.

Extension

3 The suffixes **ship**, **hood** and **ness** have been mixed up in these words. Write each word correctly.
Do it like this: *parentness – parenthood*

a) sadship

b) girlness

c) friendhood

d) boyship

e) darkhood

f) worness

g) leaderhood

h) coarseship

i) usefulship

j) childness

k) fellowhood

l) carelesshood

m) sharpship

n) manness

o) kinghood

Test your spelling!

Look at the words.
Say them aloud.
Cover the words.
Write them from memory.
Check your spellings.

shy**ness**

sharp**ness**

dark**ness**

tired**ness**

girl**hood**

boy**hood**

child**hood**

friend**ship**

leader**ship**

hard**ship**

43

Unit 21 Suffixes -ic and -ive

Key to spelling

A **suffix** is a **group of letters** that may be added to the **end** of a word. When you add a suffix it **changes** the **meaning** or **job** of the **root** word.

attract + ive = attract**ive**

angel + ic = angel**ic**

Practice

1 Join up each root word with the word that can be made from it. Write the pairs of words in your book.

act	secretive
elude	expensive
impulse	active
secret	dismissive
express	elusive
expense	responsive
dismiss	impulsive
response	expressive

2 Join up each root word with the word that can be made from it. Write the pairs of words in your book.

metal	volcanic
athlete	magnetic
volcano	metallic
hero	energetic
magnet	athletic
giant	sympathetic
energy	gigantic
sympathy	heroic

Extension

3 Write down the **ive** words from question 1 with:

a) 2 syllables

b) 3 syllables

4 Write down the **ic** words from question 2 with:

a) 3 syllables

b) 4 syllables

5 Choose three **ive** words.
Write the meaning of each word.
Use a dictionary if necessary.

6 Choose three **ic** words.
Write the meaning of each word.
Use a dictionary if necessary.

Test your spelling!

Look at the words.
Say them aloud.
Cover the words.
Write them from memory.
Check your spellings.

class**ic**

hero**ic**

volcan**ic**

athlet**ic**

electr**ic**

act**ive**

pass**ive**

attent**ive**

attract**ive**

expens**ive**

Unit 22 Suffix -ous

Key to spelling

The suffix **ous** at the end of words sounds like **us**.

poison**ous**

nerv**ous**

poison (noun) + ous (suffix)

nerve (noun) + ous (suffix)

Sometimes the **spelling** of the **root word** remains **unchanged**.

Sometimes the spelling of the **root word changes** slightly.

Practice

1 Make some words. Write the words you make in your book.

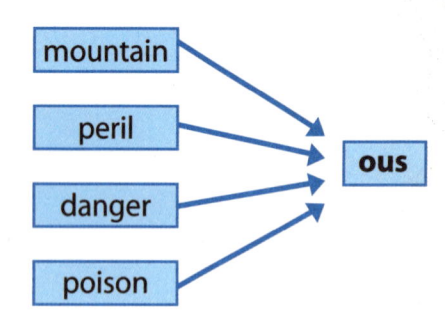

mountain → ous
peril → ous
danger → ous
poison → ous

2 When the noun ends in a **consonant + y** we change the **y** to **i** before we add the **ous**.

Add **ous** to each of these nouns. The first one has been done for you.

a) fury + ous = *furious*

b) glory + ous =

c) mystery + ous =

d) envy + ous =

e) victory + ous =

f) luxury + ous =

Extension

3 Copy these sets of suffix sums. Then write a rule for each set and say what you have discovered about the way the spelling of the root word changes when **ous** is added.

Set A

fame + ous = famous

adventure + ous = adventurous

Set B

humour + ous = humorous

vigour + ous = vigorous

Set C

fable + ous = fabulous

miracle + ous = miraculous

Set D

mischief + ous = mischievous

Test your spelling!

Look at the words.
Say them aloud.
Cover the words.
Write them from memory.
Check your spellings.

danger**ous**

joy**ous**

poison**ous**

furi**ous**

envi**ous**

mysteri**ous**

fam**ous**

humor**ous**

fabul**ous**

mischiev**ous**

Unit 23 Prefixes fore- and over-

Key to spelling

A **prefix** is a **group of letters** that may be added to the **beginning** of a word. When you add a prefix it **does not change** the **spelling** of the **root** word, but it **does change** its **meaning**.

forehead

The prefix **fore** means **before** or **in front of**.

overeat

The prefix over means **over** or **beyond**.

Practice

1 Make some words. Write them in your book.

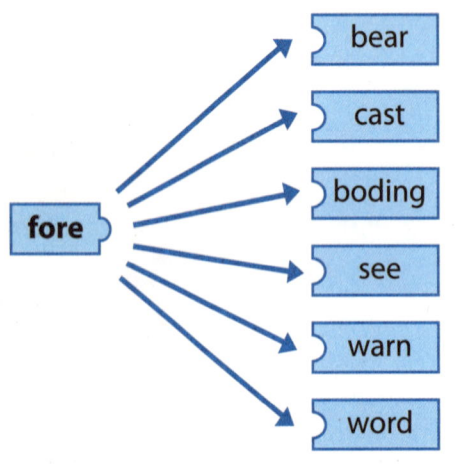

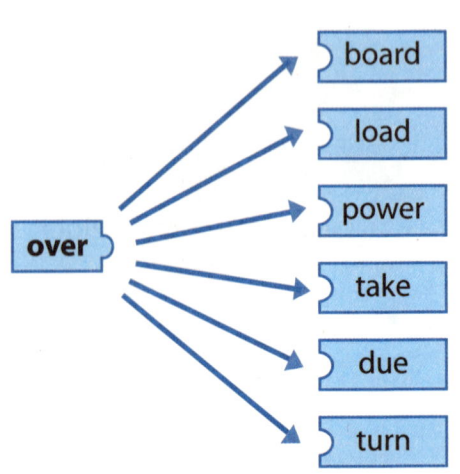

fore → bear, cast, boding, see, warn, word

over → board, load, power, take, due, turn

2 Take the prefix off each word. Write the root word you are left with.
Do it like this: ~~over~~power = power

a) overpower   b) forewarn   c) overdue   d) forebear
e) foresee   f) overtake   g) foreword h) overboard
i) foreboding j) overturn   k) forecast l) overload

Extension

3 Match each **fore** word with its meaning. Use a dictionary if necessary.

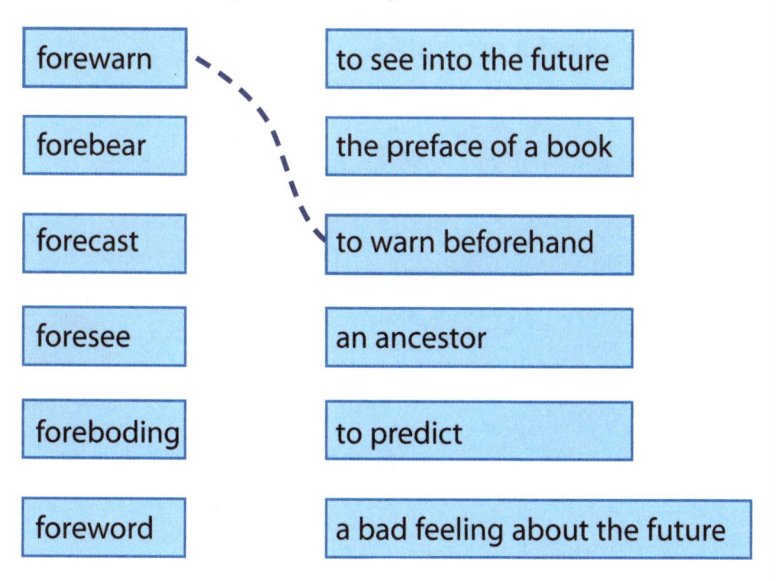

forewarn	to see into the future
forebear	the preface of a book
forecast	to warn beforehand
foresee	an ancestor
foreboding	to predict
foreword	a bad feeling about the future

4 Match each **over** word with its meaning. Use a dictionary if necessary.

overturn	to load or fill too much
overtake	to turn over or upset
overload	to be late
overpower	over the side of a ship
overdue	to overcome by greater strength
overboard	to catch up with and go past

Test your spelling!

Look at the words.
Say them aloud.
Cover the words.
Write them from memory.
Check your spellings.

foremost

forefather

foreground

foretell

forestall

overdo

overflow

overthrow

oversight

overcrowded

Unit 24 Extending words

Key to spelling

We can make some words longer by adding **prefixes** to the beginning and/or **suffixes** to the end of them.
The letters **al** may be used as either a **prefix** or a **suffix**.

Take care! When you use **al** as a prefix or suffix you only use one **l**.

alone
al + one

music**al**
music + al

Practice

1 Make some words by adding the prefix **al**.

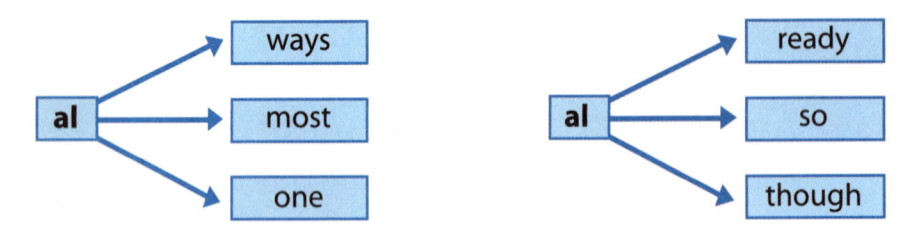

al → ways
al → most
al → one

al → ready
al → so
al → though

2 Write the words you made in alphabetical order.

3 Change these nouns into adjectives by adding the suffix **al**.

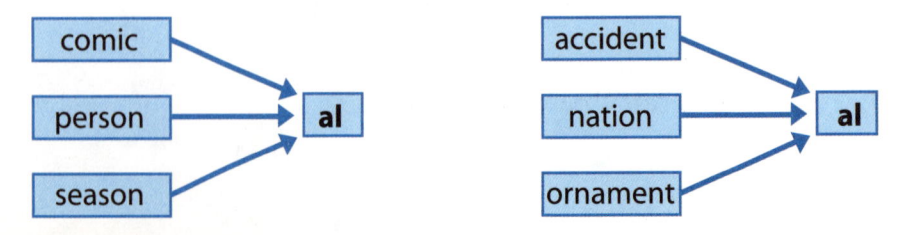

comic → al
person → al
season → al

accident → al
nation → al
ornament → al

Extension

4 Make up some sentences of your own. Use each of the words you made in question 1 correctly in your sentences.

5 Take the **al** suffix off each of these adjectives. Write the root word you are left with. Take care! Sometimes the spelling of the root word has been slightly changed. Use a dictionary if necessary.

a) original

b) tropical

c) accidental

d) occasional

e) central

f) continental

g) natural

h) tribal

i) criminal

j) universal

k) industrial

l) choral

Test your spelling!

Look at the words.
Say them aloud.
Cover the words.
Write them from memory.
Check your spellings.

also

always

almost

already

although

comic**al**

music**al**

season**al**

natur**al**

economic**al**

Unit 25 Words with common roots

Key to spelling

Being able to identify the **root word** can sometimes help us with our spelling.

to**day**    **day**light

Practice

1. Match up and write the pairs of words that contain the same root words. Underline the common root word in both.
   Do it like this: *helper   unhelpful*

invent	microphone
pressure	prevent
telephone	depressed
helping	clearly
farmer	uncomfortable
unclear	helpless
today	building
comforting	newcomer
builder	farmyard
become	knowledge
unknown	daylight

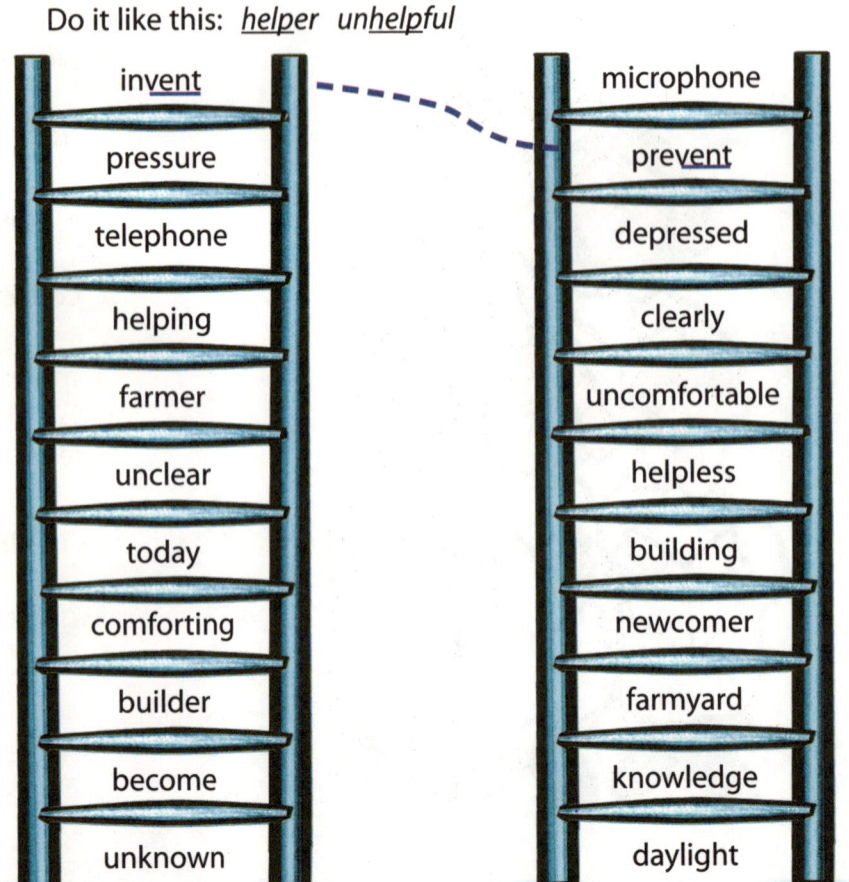

Extension

2 Add a prefix to each root word to make a longer word. The first one has been done for you.

root word	prefix + root word
like	dislike
happy	
fill	
fix	
behave	
port	
grow	

3 Add a suffix to each root word to make a longer word. The first one has been done for you.

root word	root word + suffix
dish	dishes
treat	
remark	
mix	
colour	
board	
magnet	
dark	

Test your spelling!

Look at the words.
Say them aloud.
Cover the words.
Write them from memory.
Check your spellings.

a**wake**

wakeful

out**side**

sideline

dis**play**

player

drinking

un**drink**able

re**cover**ed

dis**cover**y

Unit 26 Confusing homophones

Key to spelling

Homophones are words that **sound alike** but have **different meanings**. Some homophones are often **confused**.

The dog is wagging **its** tail because **it's** happy.

its = possessive pronoun meaning **belonging to the dog**

it's = contraction a shortened form of **it is**

There is my friend.

There usually means a **place**.

Their hands were dirty.

Their means 'belonging to them'.

They're good girls.

They're means they are.

Practice

1 Choose **it's** or **its** to complete each sentence.

a) ___ a lovely day today.

b) The dragon opened ___ mouth.

c) If ___ cold, stay indoors.

d) The monster came out of ___ cave.

2 Choose **there**, **their** or **they're** to complete each sentence.

a) _____ are three cars in the car park.

b) The children put on _____ trainers.

c) Oranges are best when _____ juicy.

d) The fishermen pulled in _____ nets.

Extension

3 Choose **to**, **too** or **two** to complete each sentence.

a) I have eaten _____ much.

b) I have _____ eyes.

c) I go _____ school each day.

d) I want _____ come with you.

e) A pair means _____ of something.

f) Don't be _____ late!

4 Choose the correct word to complete each sentence.

a) Can you _____ (here/hear) me?

b) Come over _____ (here/hear) at once!

c) _____ (We're/Were/Where) rather early.

d) _____ (We're/Were/Where) is Paris?

e) _____ (We're/Were/Where) you hurt badly?

f) I think _____ (he'll/heel) be all right.

g) I hurt my _____ (he'll/heel) when I fell over.

h) I can see _____ (your/you're) clever.

i) I can see _____ (your/you're) house.

Test your spelling!

Look at the words.
Say them aloud.
Cover the words.
Write them from memory.
Check your spellings.

its

it's

there

they're

their

your

you're

he'll

heel

heal

Unit 27 More homophones

Key to spelling

Homophones are words that **sound alike** but have **different meanings**.

a **piece** of pie

peace and quiet

Practice

1 Match up and write the pairs of homophones.

Set A	blue	nose	our	allowed	road	medal
Set B	hour	rode	blew	meddle	knows	aloud

2 Copy these sentences.
Choose the correct words to complete each sentence.

a) The pirate _____ (nose/knows) where the treasure is.

b) _____ (Blew/Blue) and yellow make green.

c) The girl _____ (blew/blue) her _____ (nose/knows) loudly.

d) The boy _____ (road/rode) his bike on the _____ (road/rode).

e) The children were not _____ (aloud/allowed) to talk _____ (aloud/allowed).

f) You must not _____ (medal/meddle) in _____ (our/hour) business.

Extension

3 Find and write eight words in the wordsearch puzzle. For each word, write another word that sounds exactly the same but has a different meaning.
Do it like this: *grown/groan*
Use a dictionary if necessary.

q	w	r	g	r	o	w	n	t	y	u	i
a	z	x	c	v	n	b	e	a	r	m	k
l	p	f	l	o	w	e	r	d	t	f	g
p	l	a	i	n	z	x	c	v	b	n	m
k	j	h	g	f	d	s	p	i	e	c	e
c	v	n	i	g	h	t	b	n	m	k	l
a	z	x	s	d	c	w	a	s	t	e	v
b	c	u	r	r	e	n	t	n	m	j	h

4 Make up some sentences of your own to show you know how to use each pair of homophones correctly.

Test your spelling!

Look at the words.
Say them aloud.
Cover the words.
Write them from memory.
Check your spellings.

peace

piece

rode

road

nose

knows

aloud

allowed

through

threw

Unit 28 Compound words

Key to spelling

A **compound word** is a word that is made up of **two smaller words** joined together.

hand   +   bag   =   handbag

Practice

1 Make these compound words.

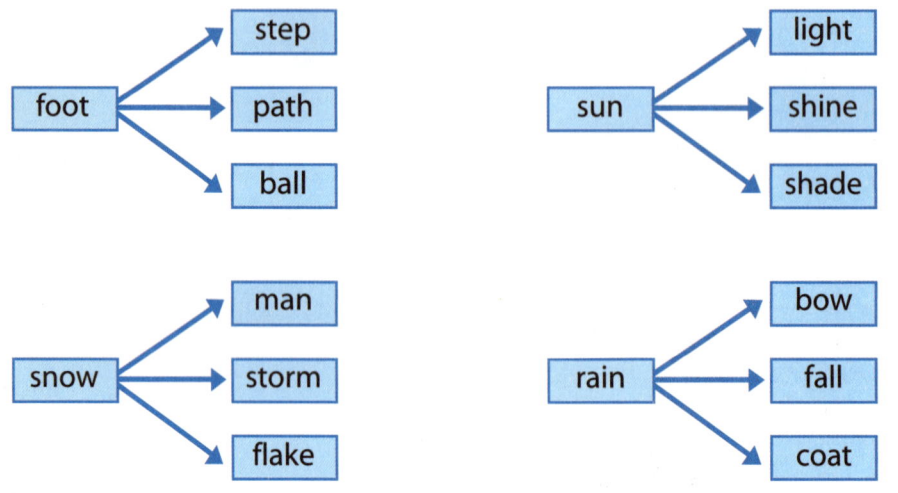

foot → step
foot → path
foot → ball

sun → light
sun → shine
sun → shade

snow → man
snow → storm
snow → flake

rain → bow
rain → fall
rain → coat

2 Break each of these compound words into two smaller words.
Do it like this: butterfly = butter + fly

a) newspaper   b) treehouse   c) bombshell   d) cupboard

e) handbag   f) waterfall   g) gooseberry   h) waistcoat

3 Choose six compound words.
Write six sentences containing them.

Extension

4 Use these word beginnings and word endings to make up as many compound words as possible.

Have a competition. See who can make up the most!

word beginnings

motor	sun	book
home	play	rain
goose	letter	tree
butter	key	sauce
tooth	water	eye
hand	news	bomb
wind	lady	hair

word endings

ache	bird	way
work	shine	coat
hole	paper	berry
case	fall	cup
mill	cuff	house
pan	box	cut
ground	sight	shell

Test your spelling!

Look at the words.
Say them aloud.
Cover the words.
Write them from memory.
Check your spellings.

afternoon

birthday

breakfast

cloakroom

cupboard

eyesight

footstep

midnight

motorway

overcome

Unit 29 Tricky words!

Key to spelling

Some words contain the **same letter strings** but they are **pronounced differently**.

cr**ash**   w**ash**

Practice

1 Copy these sets of words.
Say each word aloud.
Underline the common letter string in each word.
Circle the odd word out in each set. The first one has been done for you.

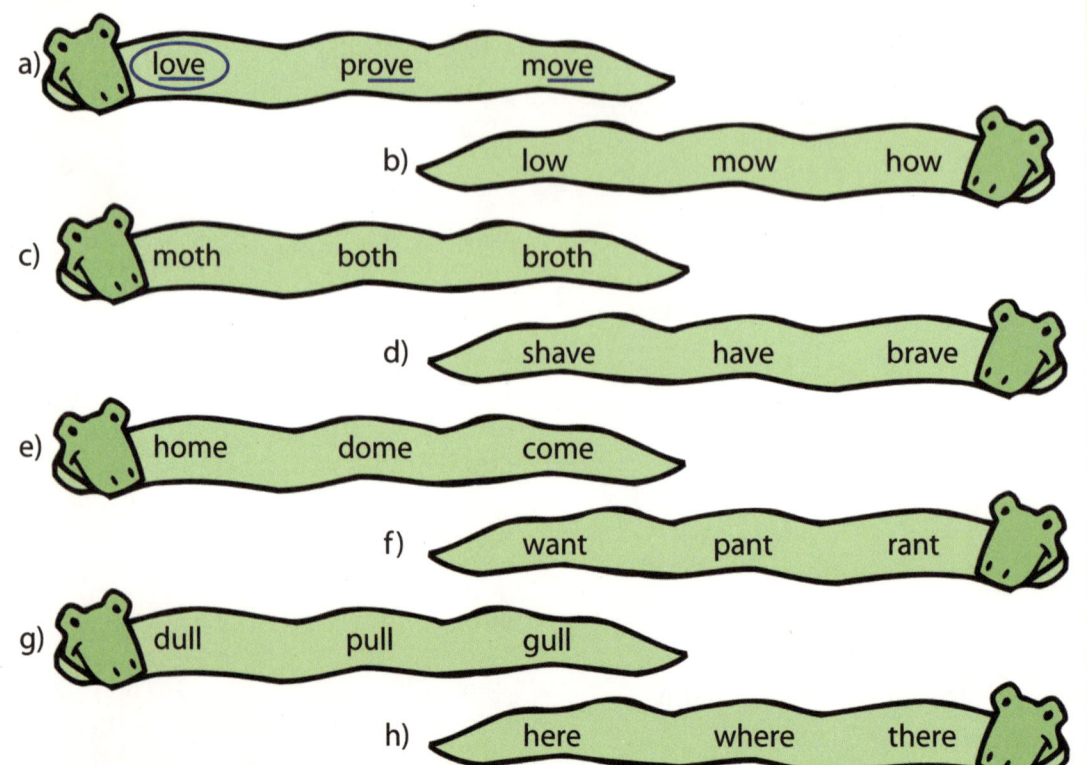

a) (love)   prove   move

b) low   mow   how

c) moth   both   broth

d) shave   have   brave

e) home   dome   come

f) want   pant   rant

g) dull   pull   gull

h) here   where   there

Extension

2 Copy these words.
Complete each word with **ough**.

a) b_____ g) n_____t

b) t_____ h) r_____

c) thr_____ i) f_____t

d) tr_____ j) en_____

e) c_____ k) b_____t

f) pl_____ l) th_____

3 Say each word you made in question 2.
Listen carefully to the sound the **ough** makes.
Write the word or words that sound like:

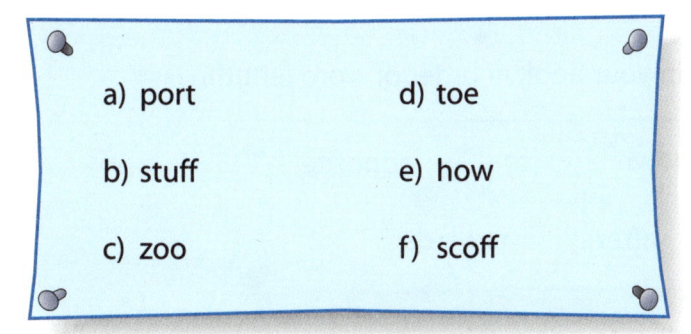

a) port   d) toe

b) stuff   e) how

c) zoo   f) scoff

4 Choose five of the **ough** words above.
Make up sentences of your own and use the words correctly in them.

Test your spelling!

Look at the words.
Say them aloud.
Cover the words.
Write them from memory.
Check your spellings.

p**our**

fla**vour**

fl**our**

j**our**ney

c**our**teous

t**ough**

thr**ough**

b**ough**

c**ough**

th**ough**

Unit 30   High frequency words

Key to spelling

Some types of words appear quite **frequently** in our writing.
Prepositions show us how one thing **relates** to another.

The boy is hiding **under** the table.

The boy is leaning **against** the table.

Practice

1 Write these sets of prepositions in alphabetical order.

a) from	except	near

b) without	after	past

c) until	upon	under

d) till	through	towards

2 Write these prepositions in your book in order of word length.

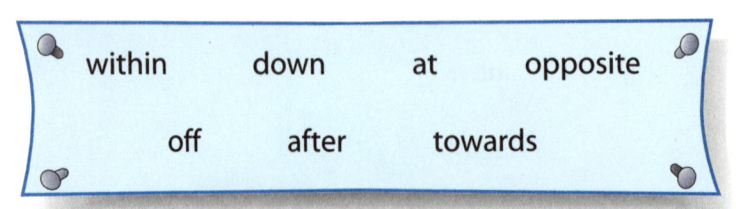

within   down   at   opposite

off   after   towards

3

aboard	beneath	towards	within	across
during	against	nearby	through	between

Which preposition contains:

a) war   b) rough   c) bet   d) ring   e) eat

f) oar   g) cross   h) gain   i) ear   j) thin

Extension

4 Make some prepositions. Write them in your book in alphabetical order.

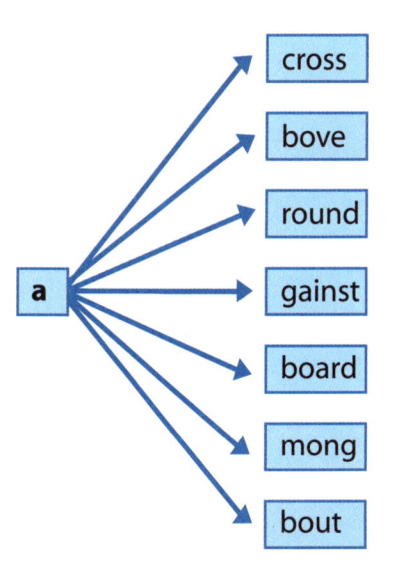

a →
- cross
- bove
- round
- gainst
- board
- mong
- bout

5 Now do the same with these.

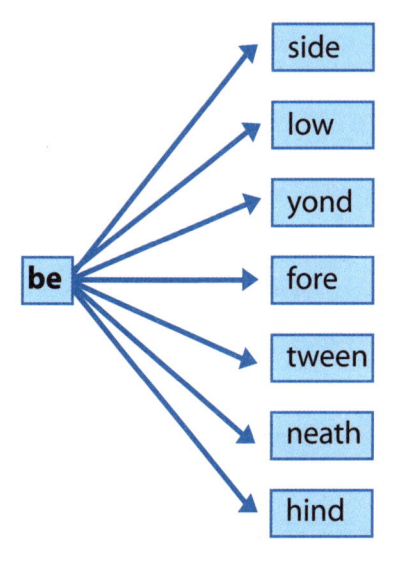

be →
- side
- low
- yond
- fore
- tween
- neath
- hind

Test your spelling!

Look at the words.
Say them aloud.
Cover the words.
Write them from memory.
Check your spellings.

along

across

above

around

below

between

before

outside

under

near

Y4 Scope and sequence

Spelling strategies

Unit	Title	Objectives	proofreading for errors	using auditory skills	using visual skills	using root words	spelling by analogy	dictionary skills	using LSCWC strategy
1	Word building (single-letter phonemes)	to identify and use single-letter phonemes for spelling (revision)		✓	✓				✓
2	Word building (multiple-letter phonemes)	to identify and use multiple-letter phonemes for spelling (revision of various phonemes)		✓	✓			✓	✓
3	Same sound/different phoneme	to identify and use phonemes with different letter strings but same pronunciations for spelling (revision **er**, **ir**, **ur**)		✓	✓			✓	✓
4	Proofreading for mistakes	to identify and use phonemes for spelling (revision **aw**, **au**, **or**)	✓	✓	✓			✓	✓
5	Same phoneme/different sound	to identify and use phonemes with the same letter strings but different pronunciations for spelling (revision **ea**, **oo**, **y**, **ow**)		✓	✓				✓
6	Check the vowel sounds	to spell words with common endings (single-syllable words with medial long vowel sounds)	✓	✓			✓	✓	
7	Working out the syllables	to discriminate syllables in reading and spelling (including two-syllable words containing double consonants)		✓	✓				✓
8	Two-syllable words (containing a long vowel)	to discriminate syllables in reading and spelling, using two-syllable words in which first syllable ends with a long vowel		✓	✓			✓	✓
9	Regular verb endings (1)	to spell verbs with regular verb endings	✓		✓	✓	✓		✓
10	Regular verb endings (2)	to spell verbs with regular verb endings	✓		✓	✓	✓		✓
11	The past tense of irregular verbs	to spell correctly the past tense of some irregular verbs		✓	✓				✓
12	Common word endings	to spell words with various common endings		✓	✓		✓	✓	✓
13	Spelling investigation (letter **k**)	to explore the occurrence of the letter **k** in words and deduce some conventions for using it correctly		✓	✓		✓	✓	✓
14	Spelling investigation (**wa** and **wo**)	to explore the occurrence of the letter strings **wa** and **wo** in words and deduce some conventions for using them correctly		✓	✓			✓	✓
15	Spelling investigation (**gu**)	to explore the occurrence of the letters **gu** in words and deduce some conventions for using them correctly		✓	✓			✓	✓
16	Spelling investigation (**se**)	to explore the occurrence of the letters **se** in words and deduce some conventions for using them correctly at the end of words		✓	✓			✓	✓
17	Suffix -**ment**	to recognise and spell some words containing the suffix -**ment**; to understand suffixes change the meaning of the root word		✓	✓	✓			✓
18	Suffixes -**tion** and -**sion**	to recognise and spell some words containing the suffixes -**tion** and -**sion**; to understand suffixes change meaning of the root word		✓	✓	✓	✓		✓
19	Suffixes -**able** and -**ible**	to recognise and spell some words containing the suffixes -**able** and -**ible**; to understand suffixes change meaning of the root word			✓	✓		✓	✓
20	Suffixes -**ship**, -**hood** and -**ness**	to recognise and spell some words containing the suffixes -**ship**, -**hood** and -**ness**	✓		✓	✓	✓	✓	✓
21	Suffixes -**ic** and -**ive**	to recognise and spell some words containing the suffixes -**ic** and -**ive**; to understand suffixes change meaning of the root word		✓	✓	✓	✓	✓	✓
22	Suffix -**ous**	to recognise and spell some words containing the suffix -**ous**; to understand suffixes change meaning of the root word			✓	✓			✓
23	Prefixes **fore**- and **over**-	to recognise and spell words containing various prefixes			✓	✓	✓	✓	
24	Extending words	to use **al** to show how words may be extended and compounded by adding prefixes and suffixes			✓	✓		✓	✓
25	Words with common roots	to investigate and spell words with common roots			✓	✓			✓
26	Confusing homophones	to distinguish between the spelling and meaning of common homophones, e.g. its/it's; there/they're/their		✓	✓			✓	✓
27	More homophones	to distinguish between the spelling and meaning of some common homophones		✓	✓			✓	✓
28	Compound words	to spell some common compound words and split them into their component parts			✓	✓	✓		✓
29	Tricky words!	to spell words with common letter strings but different pronunciations		✓	✓			✓	✓
30	High frequency words	to read and spell common high frequency words grouped thematically		✓		✓	✓	✓	